Dear Parent:
Your child's love of reading starts here!

Every child learns to read in a different way and at his or her own speed. Some go back and forth between reading levels and read favorite books again and again. Others read through each level in order. You can help your young reader improve and become more confident by encouraging his or her own interests and abilities. From books your child reads with you to the first books he or she reads alone, there are I Can Read Books for every stage of reading:

SHARED READING
Basic language, word repetition, and whimsical illustrations, ideal for sharing with your emergent reader

BEGINNING READING
Short sentences, familiar words, and simple concepts for children eager to read on their own

READING WITH HELP
Engaging stories, longer sentences, and language play for developing readers

READING ALONE
Complex plots, challenging vocabulary, and high-interest topics for the independent reader

ADVANCED READING
Short paragraphs, chapters, and exciting themes for the perfect bridge to chapter books

I Can Read Books have introduced children to the joy of reading since 1957. Featuring award-winning authors and illustrators and a fabulous cast of beloved characters, I Can Read Books set the standard for beginning readers.

A lifetime of discovery begins with the magical words "I Can Read!"

Visit www.icanread.com for information
on enriching your child's reading experience.

For Ezzy and Levon

DuKE

RoXy

Buddy

I Can Read Book® is a trademark of HarperCollins Publishers.

Library of Congress Control Number: 2015935858
ISBN 978-0-06-235706-9 (trade bdg.) — ISBN 978-0-06-235705-2 (pbk.)

The artist used Adobe Illustrator to create the digital illustrations for this book.
Design by Erica De Chavez. Hand-lettering by James Horvath.

16 17 18 19 20 LSCC 10 9 8 7 6 5 4 3 ❖ First Edition

James Horvath

Build, Dogs, Build

A Tall Tail

Max   Spot   Spike

HARPER
An Imprint of HarperCollinsPublishers

Get moving, crew.

We're heading downtown.

An old building there

needs to come down.

Time to get rolling.

Duke just got a call.

Load up the bulldozer

and the big wrecking ball.

Here's the building,

all crumbled and cracked.

We'll knock it down quickly

with a couple of whacks.

The crane is in place.

The angle's correct.

Get the ball swinging.

Wreck, dogs, wreck!

With a BOOM the ball
goes right through the wall.
Stand clear now—
the building is starting to fall.

The bulldozer clears

piles of rubble

and bricks and concrete

without any trouble.

The dump truck carries
load after load.
Fill it to the top,
then head down the road.

Start digging trenches

to run all the pipes

for water and drains,

many sizes and types.

Grab shovels and rakes—
there's concrete to pour.
This building is going
to need a good floor.

15

Here comes the steel!

Each piece looks the same.

Let's weld them together

and build a tall frame.

Look out, dogs!

Watch out for that glass!

Oh no. Too late.

The truck's going to crash!

Balls bouncing up.

Balls bouncing down.

Balls, balls, balls
flying all over town.

Let's take a quick break

and a nice, big stretch.

While we gather the balls, we can

fetch, dogs, fetch!

The excitement is over,
and we've all had fun.
But we still have pipes
and wires to run.

23

The building is bare,
with strong steel for bones.
We'll need mortar and bricks,
concrete and stones.

This crew is the best,

each dog highly skilled.

Let's keep going higher.

Build, dogs, build!

The windows are lifted
and swung through the air,
then put into place
and set with great care.

The finish work starts.

There's more to install.

Windows and stairs,

ceilings and walls.